REAL BLOCK BOYS

KALIM SHERIF

Table of Content

1. **Preface** 4
2. **Basic Terminology** .... 4.
   - 2.1 Basic terminology 5
   - 2.2 Summary 5
3. **Introduction to cryptocurrency** 8
   - 3.1 What is cryptocurrency in simple words? 10
   - 3.2 History of digital currencies 10
   - 3.3 How cryptocurrency works 10
   - 3.4 Developing cryptocurrencies 10
   - 3.5 Types of cryptocurrencies 11
   - 3.6 Cryptocurrency exchanges 13
   - 3.7 Mining cryptocurrencies 19
4. **Crypto and wealth management** .... 22.
   - 4.1 Trading cryptocurrency 24
   - 4.2 Cryptocurrency investing 24
   - 4.3 Cryptocurrency transactions 25
   - 4.4 Wallets 25
   - 4.5 ICOs 27
5. **Crypto ecosystem** 30
   - 5.1 Smart contracts 30
   - 5.2 DApps 30

	5.3 Forks………………………………………………………………………31
	5.4 Airdrops……………………………………………………………….32
	5.5 Fees……………………………………………………………………32
	5.6 Bots…………………………………………………………………….33
	5.7 Order type……………………………………………………………..33
6	**The Blockchain network**……………………………………………….35
	6.1 what is Blockchain?...35
	6.2 What Blockchain is not……………………………………………….36
	6.3 Why is it needed and what problems it solves?......................................38
	6.4 Major components of Blockchain and their purpose…………………….44
	6.5 Limitations of Blockchain…………………………………………….45
	6.6 Career opportunities in the Blockchain sphere and the skills necessary……………47
7	**Current situation and Possible future of cryptocurrencies**……………………….52
	7.1 Legality…………………………………………………………………52
	7.2 Taxes……………………………………………………………………56
	7.3 Rules and regulations ………………………………………………….59
	7.4 Possible future of cryptocurrencies…………………………………….65

1 preface

This e-book is going to be an introductory text about cryptocurrencies. It will cover the basics of cryptocurrencies, its current situation as well as its possible future. I believe that the book will serve as a companion for a crypto newbie and for hobbyists too. Topics covered in the book include an introduction to cryptocurrency, crypto and wealth management, crypto ecosystem, the Blockchain network, mining cryptocurrency and lastly, the current situation and possible future of cryptocurrencies.

2 basic terminology

2.1 Basic terminology

There are a few key terms that need to be understood at the beginning of this book before we can continue. This is only a partial list of all terms that will be used throughout this book, but these keywords are important to know before we begin the main narrative of this text.

Exchange

These are websites where the buying and selling of crypto-currencies take place.

Fiat

These are government-issued sums of money and a good example is the US dollar.

Whale

This is any person that owns a huge amount of crypto-currency.

Limit order

They are orders that are placed so as to buy or sell a cryptocurrency when the price meets a certain amount. You can also say that they are the number of crypto-currencies either sold or bought after traders place their market orders.

Bullish

it is a price increase expectation

Bearish

It is a price decrease expectation

Altcoin

This is any crypto-currency other than Bitcoin or Ethereum, though some people claim that Ethereum is an altcoin.

Tokens

This is the currency of other projects built on the Ethereum network. Some common examples are GNT – Golem, REP – Augur, BAT – Basic Attention Token, ICN – Iconomi.

ICO

It is the acronym for Initial Coin Offering and it is essentially crowdfunding on the Ethereum platform.

Stable coin

It is a cryptocurrency with extremely low volatility that can be used to trade against the overall market.

FOMO

This one is the acronym for Fear of Missing Out and it is the overwhelming feeling that you need to get on the crypto wagon when the prices start to skyrocket.

Blockchain

Ethereum falls under this classification of this technology, it is defined as a distributed ledger that is secured by cryptography. Though everyone can access and read them, their data can only be updated by the owners. The data is copied across thousands and thousands of computers worldwide instead of residing on a single centralized server.

Node

This is defined as a computer which possesses a copy of the Blockchain and is constantly working to maintain it.

Mining

it is the process of attempting to solve the next block and it requires a lot of computer processing power to work smoothly and is rewarded with ether.

Mining Rig

It is a computer that is specially designed for the sole purpose of processing proof-of- work Blockchain such as Ethereum. It is common for them to have multiple high-end graphics processors (GPUs) so as to increase their processing power.

Fork

A situation where a Blockchain divides into two separate chains and it generally happens when new rules are built into the Blockchain code.

Pow

Acronym for Proof-of-Work and it is the current consensus algorithm being applied by Ethereum.

PoS

Proof-o-stake, it is the proposed future consensus algorithm to be used by Ethereum. People that ETH will be able to 'lock up' their ether for a short amount of time in order to vote and generate network consensus, the plan is that these stakeholders will be rewarded with ETH by doing so.

software wallet

it is storage for crypto-currency that exists purely as software files on a computer, they are generated for free from a variety of sources.

Hardware wallet

It is a device that can securely store cryptocurrency. They are often regarded as the most secure way of holding way to hold crypto-currency.

Smart contract

It is code that is deployed onto the Ethereum Blockchain, often directly interacting with how money flows.

Dapp

Decentralized Application. This refers to an application that uses an Ethereum smart contract as it's back-end code.

2.2 summary

People are slowly embracing **cryptocurrencies** as an alternative for **fiat** money, several **exchanges** have been created to conduct the selling and buying of **altcoins**. Just like in any other business, we have large stakeholders called **whales** who place very high **limit orders.** The trends tend to be very unpredictable, sometimes we have **bearish** and other times we have a **bullish**. During the **mining** process, which makes use of **mining rigs**, you either earn a **token** or a coin. **ICOs** happen to be the main funding strategy for most crypto projects and the trading of a **stable coin** is very profitable and most traders are very hands-on due to **FOMO. The blockchain** is key in crypto as the ledgers are dependent on the technology, every **node** in the system counts. Currently, the coins operate on **Pow** but they may soon be based on **PoS** system. Coins once bought or mined are stored in either a **hardware wallet** or a **software wallet**. As at now, **smart contracts** are the most intriguing applications of Blockchain but that does not mean that the other **DApps** are not essential. Indeed, these new coins are quite an interesting invention.

3 Introduction to cryptocurrency

3.1 What is cryptocurrency in simple words?

Cryptocurrency is a digital virtual currency which is intended to be used as a medium of exchange, it operates independently of a central bank and is used all over the globe.

3.2 History of digital currencies

The creation of Bitcoin in 2009 marked the birth of the first digital currency to achieve widespread adoption across the globe. However, the concept of a secure digital currency has been around since the 1980s and there have been many previous attempts that directly inspired Satoshi Nakamoto's creation of Bitcoin.

In 1982, David Chaum released the paper Blind Signatures for untraceable payments in which he outlined an alternative to the electronic transactions hitting retail stores at the time. His paper is one of the very first proposals of digital currency in history. Later on Nick Szabo, the inventor of smart contracts proposed Bit Gold which was an attempt to create a decentralized digital currency though it wasn't implemented, it is considered a direct precursor to Bitcoin. Hash-cash famous in 1997 and the 1998 B-money are some other previous attempts before Bitcoin.

3.3 How cryptocurrency works

Cryptocurrencies are released to the world through a process known as mining, where you must attempt a computational puzzle known as a hash before you can mine the currency. People all over the world compete to be first to solve a hash every day in hopes of receiving either a block reward or the amount of crypto they mined. You can also buy and acquire cryptocurrency, after which you are given a digital key to its address. Using this address, you can validate or approve transactions.

Cryptocurrencies also make use of open and closed source wallets which produce and keep coin keys on your computer. A good example is the multy.io crypto wallet which is very easy to use, secure, makes use of the best UI and UX and it has multiple Blockchain support. Once in your wallet, they operate like fiat currency, as the buying and selling are rather straight forward.

3.4 Developing cryptocurrencies

I believe that you have come across Bitcoin, or Ethereum and probably even Ripple. There are over a thousand coins and token available. People are coming up with new coins on a daily basis, so why not add to the pack? Walk with me and I believe that after you are done with this article you will be able to create a cryptocurrency.

First of all, there are three requirements, these are

- **You need a brilliant idea** because creating a coin for the sake of creating a coin is bound to fail, you need to have a purpose if you want to succeed.
- **You need to earn peoples' trust,** you are required to build and maintain a crypto community.

- **You require coding and crypto security understanding,** even though you always have the option to hire talent, it is essential to know how your coin is going to work.

What do I need to create a cryptocurrency?

Creating a coin is costly and it takes a lot of time not to mention you need an incredible team of developers as it involves creating your own Blockchain from scratch. Below is a list of what you need to create a coin from scratch:

1. Initial coin offering, this is a way to raise money for crypto projects investors receive tokens and fund the project
2. Think about how the app will assist in the industry you are aiming. You need to think about a tangible problem and how Blockchain technology can resolve it, make sure that your project has real benefit.
3. Make sure you have a resilient development team who you can trust to do a good job. Make sure to hire people with years of experience working with Blockchain technology.
4. Make sure you have a strong development team to create your ICO smart contract. When investors send crypto to your smart contract it needs to send an accurate amount of your tokens to them.
5. You need a professional external audit. This is to check that your token and smart contracts are protected so you don't get hacked.
6. You need a well-written whitepaper. This is a document that presents your idea, the problem it solves, its roadmap and the technology it uses.
7. A market campaign, make use of websites, social media, pre-and-post sale community development, forums as well as the media.

8. Lastly, you need a community management team and strategy. You will need a place which your community can converse with one another and ask questions. The most prevalent app to be used for this is telegram due to its high security.

So there you have it, a summary of what you need to be able to create your own coins. Of course, you have to carry out extensive research before you embark to create your own crypto coins and it goes without saying that you need a lot of capital for this investment.

3.5 Types of cryptocurrencies

1. **Bitcoin (BTC).** Launched in 2009, it is the original cryptocurrency also the largest and most popular Blockchain network. Being the most bottle-necked tested against attackers, it is also the most secure.

Current situation

Bitcoin has experienced a rise than a fall, and recently it is undergoing a rather rapid increase. No one can explain this fluctuation, hence, it is expected that investors will question whether it is even worth it to invest in Bitcoin.

Bitcoin performance is quite outstanding; it has been able to outdo any assets or stock you might have otherwise invested in. Recently, bitcoin was starting to get sluggish but its developers doubled their efforts to make it better, and soon it was on the rise once more.

Governments have started to warm up to Bitcoin as it is taxation friendly and will reduce money laundry. Recently regulations have been put in place to ensure the safety of its users.

Benefits of Bitcoin

What are the benefits of using bitcoins?

- **Lower fraud risks for buyers.** Bitcoin acts more like digital cash that hackers cannot intercept in any possible way. Another thing is, your identity is concealed for good.
- **No risk of inflation.** With bitcoin, there is zero risk of inflation. Its system was created with the sole purpose of being finite, thus no chance of issuing excess currency.
- **Reduced transactions fees.** Transaction fees for bitcoin payments are significantly lower in comparison to the ones made for credit and debit card purchases.
- **Easy to use in any situation.** All you need is a simple memory stick and you are sorted enough for the job. You can even use the same currency in a different country without going through the pains contacting the local bank for currency conversions.

Conclusion

Just like any other investment, Bitcoin investment involves taking risks. It is essential to stay true to the basics of finances: start small, play the market wisely and patiently and you could end up with some big wins make sure you don't invest money you can't stand to lose.

2. **Ethereum (ETH).** It was launched in 2015; this coin has a built-in programming language that lets developers write computer programs, called smart contracts that can run on the Blockchain. Most initial coin offerings (ICOs) so far have been on Ethereum smart contracts.

Important things to note about Ethereum

- First of all, it is a decentralized system hence it is not controlled by any single governing entity. Being a decentralized system, it is fully autonomous, and it is not controlled by anyone. Also, it has no central point of failure as it is being run from thousands of volunteer's computers around the globe. Thus it can never go offline. Based on its decentralized nature, it essentially cuts out the need for intermediaries and the expenses associated with the involvement of a third party.

- Secondly, Ethereum took the technology behind Bitcoin and substantially expanded its capabilities. It is a whole new network, coding language, and payment system.
- It utilizes a peer-to-peer approach. Every single interaction happens between user and buyer and is supported by the users taking part in it, with no controlling authority being involved.
- Vitalic Batoriu created it in 2013.
- To obtain Ethereum, you either mine it or buy it.

What are some applications of Ethereum?

- It allows developers to build and deploy decentralized applications.
- Creating Decentralized Autonomous Organizations which operate completely transparent and independently of any intervention or any single leader.

What are some of its benefits?

- It is immune to any third party intervention hence can't be controlled by anyone at all.
- Invulnerability to fraud, corruption, and the network is tamper-proof.
- It has no history of failure.

How does the future look like for Ethereum?

Overall opinion on the future of Ethereum among cryptocurrency experts is generally favorable. However, there are many old-school financial experts who despite the extraordinary success and relative stability of both Bitcoin and Ether as well as the undeniable importance of technologies behind the projects, are still predicting their impending downfall

3. **Ripple (XRP).** Launched in 2017, this coin's developers intend for it to be a bridge that financial institutions use to settle a cross-border payment faster and more cheaply than they do now lastly, it is swift.

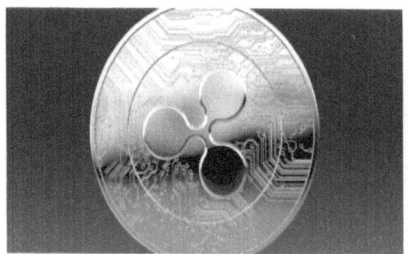

4. **Bitcoin cash (BCH).** It was launched in 2017; its creators tweaked Bitcoins software to handle larger transactions volumes.

5. **Lite coin (LTC).** Launched in 2011 and it processes transactions four times faster than Bitcoin and is very cheap.

www.shutterstock.com • 657480562

6. **Cardana (ADA).** Launched in 2017 and it emphasizes privacy and regulatory compliance. It will eventually hoist smart contracts. Uses a proof-of-stake consensus protocol and thus gobbles up less energy.

7. **Neo (NEO).** Launched in 2014, it is China's largest cryptocurrency, and it uses a fault tolerance that allows for 10,000 transactions per seconds, compared with Ethereum 15.

8. **Dash (DASH).** Launched in 2014 and formally known as coin or dark coin. It is inspired by Bitcoin but has features that sped up payment processing.

9 Nav coin Nav coin is a cryptocurrency designed to be anonymous and straightforward to use. Established in 2014 and it belongs to an older class of cryptocurrencies that came before the current wave of ICOS. It is an easy to use digital currency- run by its community. It is programmable money that lowers the cost of doing business in the web3 economy.

3.6 Cryptocurrency exchanges

These are organized and regulated financial market where cryptocurrencies, which are digital assets designed to work as a medium of exchange, are bought and sold at prices governed by the faces of demand and supply. Some common exchanges include:

Bitmex?

Bitmex is a cryptocurrency exchange as well as a derivative trading platform. It is owned and operated by HDR Global Trading Limited, which is headquartered in Hong Kong and registered in Seychelles, which was brought into being in the year 2014.

Bit-z?

Bit-z is a leading digital asset trading platform which provides both professional digital asset trading and Over the Counter services. Bit-z, founded in 2016, and its headquarter is in Hong Kong. The team behind Bit-z includes diverse professionals from industries like e-commerce, finance, gaming, and social networking, in addition to numerous members of the international digital asset industry.

Binance?

Binance is a China-based cryptocurrency exchange that grants users access to a vigorous set of trading tools, charts, and security features. It is one of the trendy cryptocurrency exchanges that offer to trade in more than 45 virtual coins including Bitcoin (BTC), Ethereum (ETH), Lite coin (LTC) and Binance Coin (BNB).

Cryptopia?

cryptopia is another cryptocurrency exchange with its coin, Dot coin. It is a cryptocurrency trading forum and marketplace platform established in New Zealand. Cryptopia provides a dynamic currency trading platform for users to get high speed and reliable processing of transactions. It enables users to deposit, trade and withdraw Lite coin, Bitcoin not to mention it gives support to more than four hundred cryptocurrencies. Users can change their New Zealand dollars to cryptocurrency by depositing their funds to NZDT and then trading for the coins, and user prefers.

Others include Coinbase, Okex, Kraken, Itnobi, and Gemini.

Common issues facing all cryptocurrencies

- **Price volatility.** Many cryptocurrencies have seen their prices drop dramatically in the recent past; this remains one of the most significant challenges cryptocurrencies face as they try to get recognition as a world currency.
- **The safety of wallets,** crypto wallets is vulnerable to hacking attacks and thefts. Weak spots have been found in hardware wallets which can be exploited, even heavily encrypted wallets are not entirely safe. By using malware, communication between the portfolios and the PCs can be intercepted. Thus compromising the privacy of the users as their funds can easily be diverted to different accounts.
- **Selfish mining,** mining pools with significant mining ratios, may mine a block and then hide it from honest miners instead of broadcasting the new block to the network. Such pools usually try to be ahead of miners and consequently get all the rewards.
- **Double spending.** Some people constitute attacks that make them benefit from using the same coin twice in the same transaction.
- **Hackers and cyber-attacks,** hackers are always targeting cryptocurrencies. Over ten percent of ICO proceeds are stolen by hackers, a percentage that amounts to the theft of up to $1.5 million in a month. Hackers are also gaining access to personal details such as addresses, phone numbers, bank details and credit card number which they use to steal crypto user's investments by directing their money to different accounts.

Protective measures

There has been an increase in the number of services aiming to make it easier for crypto-users to manage their money as well as protect it. However, there are several measures that you as an individual can take to ensure your protection. Some of these measures include:

- **Use a two-factor authentication.** If someone had access to your login details, they would also need your phone to get the 2FA code. Hence unauthorized persons are denied access to your account.
- **Do not use public WI-FI.** Use of open, free Wi-Fi to log into your account puts at the mercy of hackers and thieves.
- **Being cautious when downloading files (even on your phone).** Data that has malware attached to it and once on your, device, that malware can action some sinister commands.
- **Keeping private keys offline.** Keep the secret keys to the wallets on your computers on external storage devices for safety.

Conclusion

Even though crypto is an excellent way to invest, it presents us with quite some threats. We need to be very careful as we use this new form of technology.

3.7 Mining cryptocurrencies

What is mining?

As you probably already know, Blockchain is a digital ledger that records each and every transaction of a cryptocurrency. The Blockchain copies this transaction and sends the copies to every computer in its network.

To create or add the block to the block goes through a process of being validated by the answer to an incredibly complicated math problem. Therefore, the miners who could be individuals, groups or businesses using mining rigs to attempt and solve such problems. Such rigs consist of mining hardware as well as software which are essential in the solving of the math problems.

The first miners to solve a problem is usually rewarded with a return of the crypto coin. Once a miner finds the accurate answer to the math problem, the new block is formed and to the Blockchain while the winner earns a block reward. Every answer has to be verified by each node in the network before it is established to be valid or not.

Validating methods just like the mining process are proof-of-work this is one of the main reasons why cryptocurrency and Blockchain are considered very innovative. Giving the miners incentives ensures that crypto transactions remain secure. Not only does mining release cryptocurrency into circulation but also benefits the miners, the consumers, merchants as well as the coin itself economically.

There are a few problems associated with mining and the first one is that, with the increase in the number of the number of miners, it is becoming increasingly difficult to solve the math problems that validate the transaction. Also, you need massive amounts of electricity to power your rigs that consequently solve the problems. Lastly, too much mining actually affects the environment. But all in all, mining a good of earning money.

4 Crypto and wealth management

4.1 Trading cryptocurrency

To start trading you need to choose a cryptocurrency wallet and an exchange to trade on. Then from there, it is as simple as filling out a form and waiting for the transaction to process once your information has been verified with the exchange that you have picked.

4.2 Cryptocurrency investing

If you want to invest in cryptocurrency and not just to trade it, then you have to consider a number of things. Some of them include:

a) **Decide which kind of cryptocurrency you are interested in.**

You need to understand how the coin or its ICO operates, its history, its purpose, how long it's been in the market, its market capitalization and lastly you need to have an understanding of its underlying tech solution.

b) **Decide what type of investment you are after**

You need to make up your mind on whether you are looking to take part in a short term investment or whether you want a long term investment.

c) **Find out whether the digital asset is widely accepted and trustworthy**

Trust is crucial for prospective investors, carry out intense research and ensure that you trust the idea enough to put your money behind it.

d) Take a good look at the major crypto players so far

Seek to understand what exactly the whales did, what coins did they invest in? how much did they invest? What was the market situation then? Using this information, investment becomes rather easier and the investor is able to make better-informed decisions.

e) Make sure you invest the right amount

Only invest what you are willing to lose.

4.3 Cryptocurrency transactions

The simplest way to understand cryptocurrency transactions is to look at it like this: if I want to send some of my coins to someone else, I will first have to publish my intentions and let the nodes scan the entire coin network to validate that I haven't sent that coin to someone else already. Once that information is confirmed my transaction gets included in a block which gets attached to the previous block hence the term Blockchain. Transactions are very fast and they can't be undone or tampered with because it would mean redoing all the blocks that came after.

4.4 Wallets

What is a cryptocurrency wallet?

A cryptocurrency wallet is a secure digital wallet used to store, send, and receive digital currency like Bitcoin. Most coins have an official wallet. In order to use cryptocurrency, you will need to use a cryptocurrency wallet.

Some common types of wallets include:

Full Node Wallet: A wallet where you control your private keys and host a full copy of the Blockchain. Essentially every coin has an official wallet of this type and that can be found on the official GitHub of the site (there is often a link on the official website).

Custodial Wallet: Custodial wallets don't let you control your keys directly and most exchange wallets are custodial wallets.

Desktop Wallet: They are the most common type of wallets, you download and install them on your computer.

Mobile Wallet: A wallet that is run from a smartphone app.

Online Wallet: An online wallet is a web-based wallet. You don't download an app, but rather data is hosted on a real or virtual server. Some online wallets are hybrid wallets allowing encryption of private data before being sent to the online server.

Paper Wallet: You can print out a QR code for both public and private key. This allows you to both send and receives digital currency using a paper wallet. With this option, you can completely avoid storing digital data about your currency by using a paper wallet.

Coin-specific: A wallet that only works with a specific coin.

Network-specific: A wallet that can hold multiple tokens on a single network.

Universal: A wallet that can hold addresses from multiple coins.

software wallet

it is storage for crypto-currency that exists purely as software files on a computer, they are generated for free from a variety of sources.

Hardware wallet

It is a device that can securely store cryptocurrency. They are often regarded as the most secure way of holding way to hold crypto-currency.

4.5 ICOs

Understanding ICO.

ICO is an abbreviation for Initial Coin Offering. It means that someone offers investors some units of a new cryptocurrency or crypto-token in exchange against cryptocurrencies like Bitcoin or Ethereum.

Since 2013, ICOs are often used to fund the development of new cryptocurrencies. The pre-created token can be quickly sold and traded on all cryptocurrency exchanges if there is demand for them.

With the success of Ethereum, Initial Coin Offerings are being used more and more to fund development of a crypto project by releasing token, and then it is integrated into the plan. With this turn, ICO has become a tool that could revolutionize not just currency but the whole financial system. ICO token could become the securities and shares of tomorrow.

Some of the characteristics of an ICO include:

- Participation in a project, Decentralized Autonomous Organizations or an economy.
- Coin ICOs generally sell participation in an economy, while token ICOs sell a right of ownership or royalties to a project as well as DAO.

- Owning tokens do not always give the investor a right to vote on the direction of a project or DAO, with the rights of the investor embedded within the structure of the ICO though generally, the investor will have input throughout a projected lifespan.
- The majority of Initial Coin Offerings involve the creation of a defined number of coins or tokens before sale.
- ICOs conclude once the coins or tokens are tradable in the open market.

What are some common advantages of Initial Coin Offering?

- The project is not subject to taxation
- It does not require for intermediaries.
- There are no constraints for entry into the business.
- They have a high chance of exponential growth.
- It does not bear any geographical barriers.
- Easy validation.

Cons of ICOs

1. Attracts a lot of scammers
2. Based on pure speculation
3. Whaling time
4. Network Congestion
5. Storing the tokens
6. Government intervention

Conclusion

ICOs give you a chance to invest in new and upcoming technology, they are put up to revolutionize the industries they target, and a careful analysis of Initial Coin Offerings can help the investors board the right start-up and invest smartly.

5.0 Crypto ecosystem

5.1 Smart Contracts

A smart contract is a computer protocol intended to digitally facilitate, verify or enforce the negotiation or performance of an agreement or transaction. It runs on top of a blockchain containing a set of rules under which the parties to the contract agree to interact with each other. The security is needed for market stabilization and growth.

As explained by Vitalic Buttering, a programmer of Ethereum, in a smart card approach, an asset or currency is transferred into a program and the program runs this code and at some point it automatically validates a condition and it automatically determines whether the asset should go to one person or back to the other person or immediately refunded to the person who sent it.

Smart cards reduce reliance on trusted intermediaries (middlemen), lower transaction costs and turn legal obligations into automated processes.

Characteristics of a smart contract

i. Self- verifiable
ii. Tamper-proof
iii. Self- executable

5.2 DApps

DApps refers to decentralized applications. This is applications that run on a P2P network of computers rather than a single computer. They can also be tools or programs that run on decentralized Ethereum Blockchain. DApps have an unlimited number of participants on all sides of the market, is community-based and not controlled by any single entity.

Features of DApps

- Open Source
- Application data and records of operation must be cryptographically stored
- Decentralized
- The application must generate tokens

Dapps are used to connect buyers and sellers in marketplaces for sharing or storing files, maintaining a virtual currency and executing smart contracts in a system without ownership or censorship.

5.3 Forks

A fork is a collectively agreed upon software update. Forking is as a result of divergence in Blockchain (A blockchain splits into two branches) either temporary or permanent. Can also occur due to a change in consensus algorithm or any other software. Can either be;

1) Temporary fork

Occurs when miners on cryptocurrency system discover a block at the same time resulting into two split competing blockchains.

2) Soft Fork

A soft fork is a software upgrade that is backward compatible with previous versions of the software. They follow the old set of consensus rules and the new ones. Blocks produced by nodes conforming to the old set of consensus rules violate the new set of consensus rules and are therefore made stale by upgrading the mining majority.

3) **Hard Fork**

A hard fork is a permanent divergence from the previous version of a Blockchain. All old nodes accept blocks created by new nodes. A software upgrade that is not compatible with the previous versions of the software. All users are required to upgrade to the latest version of the software in order to continue verifying and validating new blocks of transactions.

5.4 Airdrops

Airdrop is a procedure through which a Blockchain project distributes free tokens to community members; a large number of wallet addresses. For many Blockchain startups, airdrops provide a way of gaining attention and new followers resulting in a strong user base.

It is a very effective marketing strategy for creating a large awareness. They are also used to reward any early new investors.

5.5 Fees

A Blockchain fee is a transaction fee charged on users when performing bitcoin transactions. The fee is collected to reward miners for maintaining the Bitcoin network.

The fee is used to speed up transactions and one needs to pay the Blockchain fee to ensure the bitcoin transfers arrive in a timely manner.

The lower the Blockchain fee, the lower the transactions priority in the Bitcoin network.

5.6 Bots

A crypto bot is a tool that can execute trading decisions according to a tailored algorithm.

Cryptocurrency bots can be classified as either off the shelf or custom built. Off the shelf are preferred by traders who don't program and have an inbuilt algorithm and a trading strategy implemented by the developer.

Custom built is used by traders with programming knowledge and can modify it as desired.

Bots give the traders the ability to trade and monitor their positions in a customized way so that they don't have to be constantly worried about their next move. Bots set to a predefined set of rules can result in huge profits.

The bots are dependent on internet connection and require regular maintenance.

5.7 Order Type

There are four basic types of trades in cryptocurrency.

    i. **Market Order**

It is the simplest when you buy or sell via a market order, you buy or sell the cryptocurrency at the market price plus an immediate fee if applicable. One buys or sells at the current price. Market orders are best when there are many buyers and sellers so as to avoid losses.

ii. **Limit entry order**

Also referred to as buy/sell limit. A type of order is placed to buy below the current market price or sell above the current market price. You set the price you want to buy/sell it. The order is executed when a buyer /seller wants your coins. Limit orders aren't subject to slippage

Setting limits too high /low can make one miss the opportunity of filling an order.

iii. **Stop Order**

A stop order means to execute a trade at a specific price. Once the stop order is reached the trade turns into a market order. Stop orders can experience slippage where you buy and sell at a low/high price without intending to.

iv. **Stop Limit Order**

Also referred to as the Stop Entry Order. A limit order is created at a specific price. Once a stop price is reached it turns into a limiting order. Used when one wants to open a buy trade above the current market price or a sale price below the current market price. Used when the estimation of the market price trend is known.

v. **Stop loss order**

Used to prevent a huge loss when the market price moves to an unexpected turn as compared to the trader's analysis of the market price expectations. Used after we open the trade using the other types of orders and continues to apply until the trading position is covered.

6 The Blockchain network

6.1 what is Blockchain?

The blockchain is a digital ledger in which transactions made in bitcoin or another cryptocurrency are recorded chronologically and publically.

Some key characteristics of Blockchain.

- **It has increased network capacity.** The most outstanding thing about Blockchain technology is how it improves the ability of the whole network. Therefore, several computers have been able to work together which offers excellent power than a few of the devices where the things are centralized.

- **Better security.** Blockchain technology has better protection since the chances of shutting down the system are quite slim. Bitcoin, an application entirely based on Blockchain technology, for example, has never been hacked. The Blockchain is secured by some computers called nodes which are almost impossible to cut.

- **it has increased the speed of settlement.** Traditional bank systems can be slow due to the settlement time which generally takes days to proceed. Blockchain can settle money transfer at breakneck speeds saving financial institutions a lot of time and money as well provide convenience to customers.

- **Decentralized system.** It gives you the power to store your assets in a network which further access using the internet; an asset can be anything like a contract a document or so. The Blockchain is thus such an essential tool for decentralized the web.

6.2 What Blockchain is not

[1] Blockchain is not Bitcoin: Bitcoin is an unregulated, shadow currency – often termed a "cryptocurrency". Whilst Bitcoin was the first Blockchain application, it has fundamental differences from a business Blockchain. For example, a business Blockchain usually prioritizes identity over anonymity and uses the selective endorsement of transactions in place of computationally-intensive proof of work.

[2] Blockchain is not (yet) mature: Gartner stated in their 2016 report that Blockchain is at the peak of inflated expectations on their hype cycle. They say it's some 5 to 10 years from the plateau of productivity, which I regard as conservative for some use cases. Problem is, with all the hype, it's easier to think Blockchain for business is more mature than it is. A sense of reality must be maintained, especially when seeking out the use case for a Blockchain first project.

[3] Blockchain is not a product: we refer to Blockchain as a fabric (like middleware, or plumbing) that can be used to build an exciting array of business solutions. Block chain's utility comes from an appropriate set of applications built on top of it.

[4] Blockchain is not needed when there is no business network: the existence of a business network is the mandatory test for a Blockchain use case. Quite simply, with no business network means Blockchain is overkill, and probably a distributed database would be a more appropriate (and more mature) solution.

[5] Blockchain is not a transaction processing system replacement: Blockchain can transform transactional processing across a business network for sure, but ONLY when one or more additional criteria are met – specifically:

- A business network, assets & transactions
- Multiple participants to verify transactions
- To know who's done what and when
- Trusted transactions
- A single view of truth, shared cross network

If none of these criteria are important, or our customers are happy with the levels provided by their current solution, then a Blockchain replacement is not needed.

[6] Blockchain is not a distributed database replacement: Blockchain complements distributed database technology, with appropriate information partitioning between the two. And as cited in [4] above, a distributed database is likely a better solution where a business network is not involved.

[7] Blockchain is not a secure messaging replacement: there are many excellent secure messaging solutions which are invaluable in integrating together disparate business systems. Blockchain technology is complementary – indeed has much to learn far from secure messaging systems – and is certainly not a replacement for them!

[8] **Blockchain is not just about currency**: whilst Blockchain is an excellent choice for a regulated digital currency, it can be used keep a trusted audit trail of ownership of a vast range of asset types – both tangible (house, car, diamond, antique violin) and intangible (digital music, digitized video, financial instrument, document, digital goods) assets. This makes for a highly diverse choice of Blockchain use cases.

[9] **Blockchain is not usually suited for high volume, low-value transactions**: as Blockchain for business matures, fabric developers will turn to non-functional requirements including transaction throughput. In the near term, the technology remains better suited to low volume high-value transactions, because of the additional qualities of service that a distributed processing system provides.

[10] **Blockchain is not (necessarily) anonymous**: depending on the choice of fabric, Blockchain can support anonymous transactions across an "untrusted" network. However, Blockchain for business prioritizes identity and trust over anonymity.

6.3 Why is it needed and what problems it solves?

Applications of Blockchain

- **Smart contracts**

They are digital self-executable agreement that business parties sign in cooperation with each other's terms and conditions. Smart contracts applications include financial agreement, health insurance, real estate property documents as well as crowdfunding. They are very safe as they are not prone to alteration and hacking.

- **It promotes fair government election**

Blockchain smart contracts provide a modern system that eradicates fraud. Entry in the smart deals will allow transparency and security while maintaining the privacy of the voters thus enabling fair elections.

- **The other application is identity management.**

The distributed ledger technology users in Blockchain offers you advanced method of public-private encryption using which you can prove your identity and digitize your documents. Hence you can safely conduct online transactions.

- **Information storage.**

Corporations, as well as individuals, can store information ranging from car logs, business transactions to medical records. This information cannot tamper with thanks to the encryption of data thus its users are assured of high-class privacy.

- **It is essential in defrauding charities.**

Blockchain technology when adopted into the charitable organizations' systems, keeps companies accountable thus eliminating embezzlement of funds and contributions.

- **It encourages ethical business practices.**

The technology makes possible to track every transaction with complete transparency hence making it easier to observe all its users' activities. Too bad for illegal businesses as they will have no choice but to engage in more ethical practices and help build the economy.

- **It Enables a Sharing Economy**

1. **Decentralized marketplaces**. Here buyers and sellers interact directly; people are free to register any products on the platform which are visible to all the other users connected to the network. Once the buyer and seller have settled on the price, the buyer is expected to release the funds. Only if there is an issue between the two does there arise a need for a third party.

2. **Decentralized carpooling platforms**. Uber based on the blockchain whereby blockchain deals with all the codes that handle the sharing of rides. It rewards drivers contributing to the platform. The more the driver's contribution, the better the reward.

3. **Decentralized applications**. Projects such as Sharing have managed to merge all existing sharing platforms into one app which users can execute transactions efficiently across all of these platforms. saving you the trouble of downloading all the sharing apps yet still be able to access all these services. Even when traveling abroad you don't have to worry about finding locally relevant sharing apps as such are similar and global.

4. **Decentralized organizations**. Such organizations are usually administered collectively, no need for hierarchical structure. Not only are such organizations dematerialized but also decentralized, users qualify as both contributors and shareholders of their platforms and the payment is fair.

- **Blockchain applications in Business**

I know you are probably reading and Thinking "fine I have understood what Blockchain is and even explored some of its key characteristics, but how does it apply to me as a business person?" Worry not for we are about to explore that together, they include:

1. **Smart contracts**

They are self- automated computer programs that can carry out the terms of any contract. These contracts run exactly as programmed without any possibility of downtime, censorship, fraud or third-party interference. Businesses will be able to use smart contracts to bypass regulations and lower the costs for a subset of common financial transactions. Best of all, these contracts will be durable.

2. **Cloud storage**

This is another application that businesses can take advantage of. Business can offer cloud storage while decreasing dependency. Instead of using excess hard drive space, users could store the traditional time 300 times over. I strongly believe that cloud storage will significantly reduce the cost of storing data for companies and personal users.

3. **Supply chain communication and proof-of- provenance**

Most of the things we purchase aren't made by a single entity but rather a chain of suppliers who sell their components to a company which assembles and sells the final product. The problem with this method is that if one of these components fails, the entire process backfires. Using Blockchain technology would proactively give digitally permanent, auditable records that show stakeholders the state of product at each value-added step thus assuring them of a smooth sail since a problem will be detected very early and solved.

4. **Paying employees**

As we know, Blockchain has its roots in cryptocurrency; it only makes sense that it could be used as an application to compensate employees. If your company normally pays wages to international workers, then incorporating Bitcoin into the payroll process could be a major cost saver.

- **Medicine**
  - A medical Blockchain company is an organization that has incorporated the Blockchain technology into the health sector. Such a company enables patients, specialists, research institutions and application developers from all over the world to collaborate in an attempt to improve the healthcare sector. Medical Blockchain companies use the Blockchain technology in several ways which include: Patient health data storage and secure mode of payment for health services. Some of the renown worldwide medical Blockchain companies are Cura, nebula Genomics, Iryo, Patiently, Guardtime, gem, chronicled, coral health and Simply vital health.

What are the benefits of medical Blockchain Companies?

The benefits that users get just by being a part of a medical Blockchain Company are quite vast. In my opinion, this is the direction our health sector should take as it has found a way to solve very many problems that hindered healthcare excellence in the past. Some of the perks of being a part of a medical Blockchain Company include the following:

1. **Patients are assured of secure storage and usage of their health records.** These companies introduce utilization of Blockchain technology to store patient's health records and maintain a single version of the patient's accurate data. To ensure that only the

patient can access their files, each patient has a unique self-sovereign identity. Data privacy is, therefore, a fundamental feature provided by these companies.

2. **Grant specialists and research organizations access to the patients' medical records.** Healthcare agents such as doctors, hospitals, laboratories, pharmacists and insurers can request permission to access and interact with medical records. Each interaction is auditable, transparent, secure and will be recorded as a transaction on the company's distributed ledger.

3. **Patients are assured of data privacy even when other parties access their records.** Medical Blockchain companies are built on permission-based Hyper ledger fabric architecture which allows varying access levels; patients control who can view their data, how much they see and for what length of time.

4. **Remote consultation service for patients.** Certified physicians provide medical services via video- consultation, Blockchain media records and electronic prescriptions. Patients and doctors from all walks of life can interact, and this service is usually available 24 hours a day.

5. **Drug adherence.** These companies use a series of outreach tools and messages supported by predictive modeling and behavioral analytics to increase the rate of drug adherence by patients.

6. **Easies the specialists' responsibility.** Not only does the Blockchain technology increase the quality of care for patients but it also reduces the physician's costs for storing patients' data hence such doctors can focus on taking care of their patients.

7. **Collaboration.** Doctors and other research entities can work together in an attempt to solve health puzzles, this promotes world peace and also improves these individuals' skills tremendously.

8. **Application monetization.** Application developers are provided with a platform where they share their inventions, and once in a while, they can sell their software and make good money out of it.

9. **Earning.** Everyone's contribution gets rewarded, the patients, the specialists, the research organization and even app developers earn rewards based on their input which makes these companies somewhat fair.

10. **Discoverability.** Especially applies to specialists, their satisfactory work is usually noticed, and once that happens, they get more and more clients hence expanding themselves globally.

6.4 Major components of Blockchain and their purpose

Blockchain can actually be thought of as the combination of several different existing technologies. While these technologies themselves aren't new, it is the ways in which they are combined and applied which brought about. There are three component technologies that make Blockchain up and they are:

- Private key cryptography

- A distributed network that includes a shared ledger

- Means of accounting for the transactions and records related to the network

To illustrate the technology of private cryptographic keys, it helps to envision two individuals who wish to conduct a transaction online. Each of these individuals holds two keys: One of these is private and one is public. By combining the public and private keys, this aspect of cryptography allows individuals to generate a secure digital identity reference point. This secure identity is a major component of Blockchain technology. Together, a public and a private key generate a digital signature, which is a useful tool for certifying and controlling ownership.

The digital signature of the cryptography element is then combined with the distributed network technology component. Blockchain technology acts as a large network of individuals who can act as validators to reach a consensus about various things, including transactions. This process is certified by mathematical verification and is used to secure the network. By combining the use of cryptographic keys with a distributed network, Blockchain allows for new types of digital interactions.

6.5 Limitations of Blockchain

It is indisputable that Blockchain has extensive applications and that it is very crucial in our financial future, however, it still has its shortcomings. Some of the current issues and limitations of Blockchain include:

1. **Complexity**

Blockchain technology involves an entirely new vocabulary, it has made cryptography more mainstream, but the highly specialized industry is chock-full of verbiage. Thankfully, there are several efforts at providing glossaries and indexes that are thorough and easy to understand.

2. **Network size**

Blockchain, like all distributed systems, is not so much resistant to bad actors as it is 'anti-fragile' – that is, they respond to attacks and grow stronger. This requires a large network of users, however. If a Blockchain is not a robust network with a widely distributed grid of nodes, it becomes more difficult to reap the full benefit. There are some discussion and debate about whether this a fatal flaw for some permission Blockchain projects.

3. **Transaction costs, network speed**

Bitcoin currently has notable transaction costs after being touted as 'nearly free' for the first few years of its existence. As of late 2016, it can only process about seven transactions per second, and each transaction costs about $0.20 and can only store 80 bytes of data. There's also the politically charged aspect of using the Bitcoin Blockchain, not for transactions, but as a store of information. This is the question of ''bloating' and is often frowned upon because it forces miners to perpetually reprocess and rerecord the information.

4. **Human error**

If a Blockchain is used as a database, the information going into the database needs to be of high quality. The data stored on a Blockchain is not inherently trustworthy, so events need to be recorded accurately in the first place. The phrase 'garbage in, garbage out' holds true in a Blockchain system of record, just as with a centralized database.

5. **Unavoidable security flaw**

There is one notable security flaw in bitcoin and other Blockchain: if more than half of the computers working as nodes to service the network tell a lie, the lie will become the truth. This is called a '51% attack' and was highlighted by Satoshi Nakamoto when he launched bitcoin. For this reason, bitcoin mining pools are monitored closely by the community, ensuring no one unknowingly gains such network influence.

6. **Politics**

Because Blockchain protocols offer an opportunity to digitize governance models, and because miners are essentially forming another type of incentivized governance model, there have been ample opportunities for public disagreements between different community sectors. These disagreements are a notable feature of the Blockchain industry and are expressed most clearly around the question or event of 'forking' a Blockchain, a process that involves updating the Blockchain protocol when a majority of a block chain's users have agreed to it. These debates can be very technical, and sometimes heated, but are informative for those interested in the mixture of democracy, consensus and new opportunities for governance experimentation that Blockchain technology is opening up.

6.6 Career opportunities in the Blockchain sphere and the skills necessary

Career opportunities in the Blockchain sphere and the skills necessary

Can you believe that Blockchain expertise captured the first position in one the latest skills index for being the hottest in the United States job market? Isn't that the craziest thing ever? Less than a decade ago very few people cared for this technology which has become such a buzz word and now a significant employer. The demand for people with Blockchain skills is quite high. Due to its many fields of application, it is looking to hire those who have skills set to navigate this new technology. Of course, just like with any other fantastic job opportunities, not everyone is cut out for these opportunities. You must have special skills that set you apart and make an employer want to entrust you with their investment.

Who is hiring?

First of all, let's explore who these potential employers are. There are four significant bosses in the crypto job market, these are:

1. **Startups** – these are independent businesses and products created since the invention of Blockchain.

2. **Legacies** – these are big companies like banks, accountancy firms as well as law offices that want to keep up with the technology.

3. **Tech firms** – these are the companies that have the most to lose in case Blockchain tech takes over the world. As they try to shift to a decentralized system, they need all the expertise they can gather.

4. **Governments -** many governments have been hiring crypto experts to advise them. Several governments are warming up to Blockchain due to its many advantages; Blockchain professionals are in high demand.

I know you are probably wondering what these jobs and careers are and if they are available, let me answer that as walk with me. Here are some of those positions

- **Blockchain developer**

Blockchain developer with the expertise to help companies explore Blockchain platforms are on high demand. Blockchain development might be the most marketable career path today because people are eager to realize all the benefits of Blockchain. These individuals require absolute attention to detail as theirs is a high ranking position.

- **Blockchain project manager**

This individual is entrusted with the responsibility of connecting Blockchain projects to experts whose duty is to develop Blockchain solutions. Blockchain project managers need to be equipped with the skills of a traditional project manager. They also need to master the technical bit to understand the technology thoroughly. Another important ability is excellent communication skills; this is essential when addressing non-technical workers, when providing useful updates or when trying to get resources from higher authorities.

- **Blockchain designer**

With the incorporation of Blockchain into so many industries, its design, as well as user interface, is becoming somewhat critical. The role of a Blockchain designer is manipulating a user interface that creates trust and is alluring to a regular user. These individuals need to be able to pay attention to detail, have an artistic touch, but most importantly they need to be hardworking as their line of work requires them to spend a countless number of hours behind their computers.

- **Blockchain quality engineer**

In any development environment, we have quality assurance engineer who tests and ensures that all areas of the project are of the required quality. In the Blockchain world, a Blockchain engineer plays a similar role by guaranteeing that all operations are of excellence in the Blockchain development environment. In other words, they conduct the testing and automation of frameworks for Blockchain. These individuals need to have a third eye as far as payment to detail is concerned because a small mistake on their part affects everyone using their technology. Excellent communication skills would also go a long way in the maintaining of good work relationships.

- **Blockchain attorney or legal consultant**

Of course, as organizations try to comprehend the adoption of Blockchain into their systems legal issues always arise. As companies launch this new technology, they are also looking for legal expertise on what considerations to make while investing. They are curious about the implications of their actions, about how to handle their finances and lastly how to manage their identity. I do not think that I need to expound on how essential attorney is to such companies. Of course, for such an individual, proper communication skills are mandatory. You also need to have a good grasp of your international law as Blockchain is tech without borders for the same reason it is advisable that such people master as many universal languages as they can.

- **Accountants**
- **Public Relations**
- **Marketers**

- **Crypto journalists**
- **Managers**
- **Crypto brokers**
- **Analysts**
- **ICO advisors**

Are these jobs available?

Did you know that there is a Blockchain job site? I bet you didn't, it is called Crypto Jobs List and it advertises vacancies in marketing, community, design and even has listings for meme specialists Intriguing right!!!!

If you want to be successful in a crypto career, try the following

1. Keep up to date with industry trends
2. Be flexible; these careers come in many forms
3. Love crypto, I feel like that one goes without saying.

Conclusion

As the Blockchain technology continues to evolve, so will it's professional opportunities. In my opinion, Blockchain is here with us to stay which means that Blockchain Expertise is likely to be in demand for years and years to come. So whether you are a techie or not, a career in Blockchain is a new and exciting opportunity worth exploring.

7 Current situation and Possible future of cryptocurrencies

7.1 Legality

For most potential investors, the action of most government officials placing regulatory measures in place to curb crypto trading is rather discouraging. The techno-phobic commoners are thinking that it must be illegal because terrorists are using it and newbies are convinced that it is crashing. It is indeed heartbreaking how people are making up their minds against a technology that they barely understand. For national governments, it is quite hard to wrap cryptocurrencies in traditional regulations but it will be such a disadvantage for everyone if they totally ban the technology. This is due to the advantages it offers which include:

- Fast and easy cross-border transactions with low fee irrespective of the amount.
- No need of Bank like infrastructure on several locations which incurs extra cost.
- Secure. (The banking industry has got its fair share of hack and fraud cases)
- Smart-contracts reducing the manual work that goes into accounting and settlement.
- Decentralized power.

Some of the main reasons for resistance against cryptocurrency include:

a) **Old Laws**

The old definition of money, commodity, or asset/property as declared in the constitution of many countries can't fathom the Digital Currency. They fail to identify Cryptocurrency as money or asset and thus they cannot classify it. The lawmakers could have never predicted this. The inability of laws to accept digital currency is a roadblock for the regulatory authorities. The nations with the right infrastructure and willingness modified their policies quickly. Others are finding it tough to give it a room.

b) Public Safety

Many countries along with the Indian Govt. are concerned about the security of public money. In case of a hack or downtime or failure of service, who will be responsible. Their question is, 'Who should we run behind in case of fraud or complaint?'. The IT acts are old; they didn't comprehend that they'll ever need to tackle crimes in decentralized applications.

c) Anonymity

Governments want to keep a record of who owns what. They need to audit the wealth of the public for numerous purposes. In Cryptocurrency it is hard to keep an account of that. Moreover, the governments do not have a trusted official body to deal with the technology.

d) Control over money

The Central Reserve Banks and Federal Banks want to exercise control over money. They will lose control over inflation/deflation in the market, the supply of currency, and liquidity in the market. The current financial system is dependent upon credit and debt; these traditional notions are not crystal clear in Cryptocurrency.

e) Regulatory bodies do not have a way to control the money

f) **The government bodies are having a rough time collecting taxes from crypto investors**

1. **Where is cryptocurrency legal?**

Some of the crypto friendly countries include The United States, Canada, Australia, The European Union, Malta, Bermuda, Switzerland, Gibraltar, Slovenia, Singapore, Estonia, Georgia, Belarus, Hong Kong, Japan, Germany, South Africa, and Nigeria.

2. **Where is cryptocurrency banned?**

Some of the countries that have said no to crypto are China, Russia, Vietnam, Bolivia, Columbia, and Ecuador.

Bitcoin Legality by Country/Regions

Below is collecting information on the legality status of Cryptocurrencies which is curated by the community. This map can be trusted as it is curated by the tech-enthusiasts and early adopters residing in those countries.

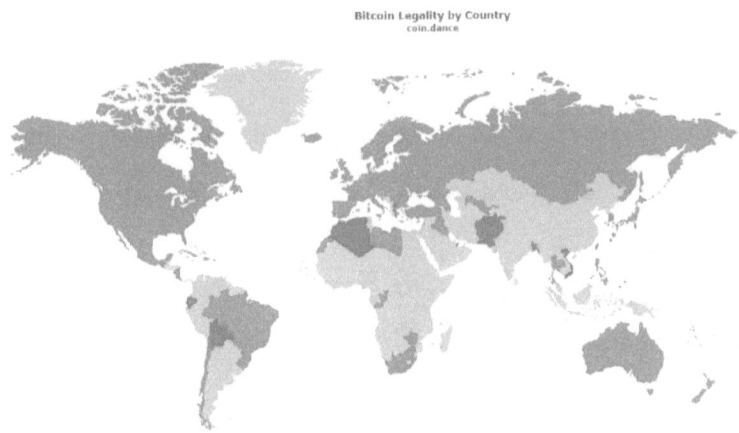

Crypto regulation world map

Green- legal/regulated

Yellow- restricted/ not-regulated

Red- illegal

Even with regulations put in place, people are still using cryptocurrencies because it is convenient, global and some simply have no idea that it is illegal in their countries. Day in day out new coins are being discovered and being adopted into fields that were only imaginable a few years ago. Such fields include paying of school fees, booking traveling tickets as well as paying hospital bills.

The Revolution Will Not Be Centralized

Which means, a written word in the government's book cannot keep a ban on Cryptocurrency.

If people want to use them, they will. The Cryptocurrency do not seek the approval of central authorities. Yet the mass adoption is not possible without the intervention of regulatory bodies.

There are both challenges and opportunities for us in the digital age. The central banks are seeing competition for the first time. The competition is good for any market. This will force them to improve the age-old financial system and to make fiat more lucrative, they may try to offer Cryptocurrency like features in them. The banks never had competitors, now they do.

The Cryptocurrencies do face deflation risk, volatility, taxation issue, lack of regulation, public awareness etc. but not the solid use cases.

7.2 Taxes

there has been such a debate on whether or not profit made on cryptocurrencies is taxed or not. Considering the anonymity nature of the currencies, taxing their traders can be quite tricky too but it is only fair that they are taxed.

IRS Notice 2014-21

The IRS addressed the taxation of virtual currency transactions in Notice 2014-21. According to the Notice, virtual currency is treated as property for federal tax purposes. This means that, depending on the taxpayer's circumstances, cryptocurrencies, such as Bitcoin, can be classified as business property, investment property, or personal property. General tax principles applicable to property transactions must be applied to exchanges of cryptocurrencies. Hence, notice 2014-21 holds that taxpayers recognize gain or loss on the exchange of cryptocurrency for other property. Accordingly, gain or loss is recognized every time that Bitcoin is used to purchase goods or services.

Determining Basis & Gain

When it comes to determining the taxation of cryptocurrency transactions, it is important for cryptocurrency owners to properly track basis. The basis is generally defined as the price the taxpayer paid for the cryptocurrency asset. Treating cryptocurrency, such as Bitcoin, as property creates a potential accounting challenge for taxpayers who use it for everyday purchases because a taxable transaction occurs every time that a cryptocurrency is exchanged for goods or services. Taxpayers must track their cryptocurrency basis continuously to report the gain or loss recognized on each crypto transaction properly. It is easy to see how this treatment can cause accounting issues with respect to everyday cryptocurrency transactions. On the other hand, the loss recognition on cryptocurrency transactions is equally complex. A deduction is allowed only for losses incurred in a trade or business or on a transaction entered into for profit. Whether Bitcoin is held for investment or personal purposes may be difficult to determine, and further guidance by the IRS on this topic is needed. Cryptocurrency values have been extremely volatile since its inception. As illustrated below, this volatility makes a significant difference in gain or loss recognition.

In sum, taxpayers must track their cryptocurrency purchases carefully. Each cryptocurrency purchase should be kept in a separate online wallet and appropriate records should be maintained to document when the wallet was established. If a taxpayer uses an account with several different wallet addresses and that account is later combined into a single wallet, it may become difficult to determine the original basis of each cryptocurrency that is used in a subsequent transaction.

The details of all cryptocurrency transactions in a network are stored in a public ledger called a "Blockchain," which permanently records all transactions to and from online wallet addresses, including date and time. Taxpayers can use this information to determine their basis and holding period. Technology to assist taxpayers in this process is being developed currently and some helpful online tools are now available.

The character of gain or loss on a cryptocurrency transaction depends on whether the cryptocurrency is a capital asset in the taxpayer's hands. Gain on the sale of a cryptocurrency that qualifies as a capital asset is netted with other capital gains and losses. A net long-term capital gain that includes gain on crypto transactions is eligible for the preferential tax rates on long-term capital gains, which is 15% or 20% for high net-worth taxpayers. Cryptocurrency gain constitutes unearned income for purposes of the unearned income Medicare contributions tax introduced as part of the Affordable Care Act. As a result, taxpayers with modified adjusted gross incomes over $200,000 ($250,000 for married taxpayers filing jointly) are subject to an additional 3.8% tax on cryptocurrency gain.

If a taxpayer acquires cryptocurrency as an investment and chooses to dispose of it by purchasing merchandise or services, any loss realized will be treated as a deductible investment loss. However, at times, it may be difficult to determine whether cryptocurrency is held for investment or personal purposes.

According to Notice 2014-21, if a taxpayer's mining of cryptocurrency is a trade or business, and the taxpayer isn't classified as an employee, the net earnings from self-employment resulting from the activity will be subject to self-employment tax. Cryptocurrency mining is defined as a computationally intensive process that computers comprising a cryptocurrency network complete to verify the transaction record, called the "Blockchain", and receive digital coins in return. Cryptocurrency mining is considered a trade or business for tax purposes, in contrast to investing in cryptocurrencies which are considered an investment. This is a crucial distinction since the taxation of investment gains or losses are subject to the capital gain/loss tax regime, whereas, business income is subject to a different tax regime. A taxpayer generally realizes ordinary income on the sale or exchange of a cryptocurrency that is not a capital asset in his hands.

The IRS's guidance in Notice 2014-21 clarifies various aspects of the tax treatment of cryptocurrency transactions. However, many questions remain unanswered, such as how cryptocurrencies should be treated for international tax reporting (FBAR & FATCA reporting) and whether cryptocurrencies should be subject to the like-kind exchange rules.

7.3 Rules and regulations

What's the Current Approach to Regulation?

It is unarguable that a lesser number of countries have constrained Bitcoin, still, most other countries permit its use. The decentralized state of Bitcoin makes it very challenging to implement constraints on Bitcoin, even in the few states that have already forbidden it. Below, is a piece of the different ways some countries are handling it.

USA

The US is yet to have a have a uniform tactic to the rule on Bitcoin at a country level. The Federal Reserve lacks a policy concerning the regulation of Bitcoin, although it has been said it is a matter that they will have to consider at some point in the forthcoming days. The Financial Crimes Enforcement Network, which happens to be an agency within the US Treasury Department, made sure to publish guidelines about cryptocurrency during the coin's onset. This suggested that even though using cryptocurrency for buying legal goods and services was not exactly illegal, the mining or trading of bitcoin and also the operation of exchanges on which Bitcoins are transacted would fall under the label of "money transmitters " and would be subject to the same Anti-Money Laundering (AML) and Know Your Client (KYC) measures as other money service businesses. FinCEN has also been convoluted in action again the Russian-domiciled Bitcoin exchange for a fissure of US AML laws, which was the first action taken against a non-US based exchange.

The US Securities and Exchange Commission (SEC) has yet to issue any regulations on Bitcoin or cryptocurrencies. However, they have issued a number of warnings about the volatility and risk of fraud in the sector, including a warning from the chairman of the SEC in November 2017 relating to the risks surrounding ICO's. The US Commodity Futures Trading Commission

(CFTC) has designated Bitcoin to be a commodity, and although the CFTC does not regulate Bitcoin directly, it does have authority in respect of commodity futures that are directly connected to Bitcoin. For example, the CFTC recently accepted a proposal by the Chicago Mercantile Exchange to allow Bitcoin and other cryptocurrencies to be cleared in the same manner as other products, which could have a major effect on the value of Bitcoin.

At a State level, there have been various approaches taken by individual States, particularly in relation to the regulation of exchanges or other money transmitters. Some States, such as New York, have made attempts to make specific licensing regimes that are applicable to cryptocurrency exchanges whereas other states, such as Texas, continue to apply existing financial laws and regulations to the use of cryptocurrencies. However, the effect of this license in New York was considered by some to be a stifling of the fintech industry's use of cryptocurrency in that State. In fact, the New York Bitlicence is currently being challenged by the Bitcoin Foundation, who are increasingly active in lobbying against large scale regulation of the industry. The Bitcoin Foundation has stated its opinion that the US government is increasing federal and state regulation of Bitcoin in the US with a view to "control and stifle the adoption and use of so-called 'virtual currencies' such as Bitcoin."

European Union

The EU has taken a more open approach to Bitcoin than the US, as well as offering less indistinctness. Indeed, the EU already had a framework to administrate the use of electronic money before the development of Bitcoin, which was adaptable to fit cryptocurrencies such as Bitcoin.

The European Central Bank has classified Bitcoin as a 'convertible decentralized virtual currency'. The European Banking Authority (EBA) has advised European banks not to trade in any cryptocurrencies until a regulatory regime was put in place. In 2016, the European Legislature agreed to set up a task force to monitor cryptocurrencies with a view to combating money laundering and violence. The European Commission has further proposed that cryptocurrency exchanges and digital wallets would be subject to directive in order to prevent tax evasion.

The current rapporteur of the first Blockchain Resolution of the European Parliament has suggested that the profits of a framework of rules in respect of the Blockchain industry would allow for companies and customers operating in the sphere to act on a level playing field. She stated that without certainty about regulation, it is unlikely that the required scalability of the technology will be able to occur. She further proposed that ICOs, for example, should be defined within their own structure, rather than any attempt be made to make it fit into the current regulatory structures of securities or commodities. This approach is in line with the view of the Bitcoin Foundation themselves, who have stated that any premature regulation of Bitcoin "might put it into a box it might not fit into later on."

China

Although lawful for individuals in China, there was a crackdown on the trading of Bitcoin in 2017, with multiple exchanges having to delay uncountable Bitcoin withdrawal services. This clampdown arrived with an increase in the Chinese media noting the risks of cryptocurrency as a tool for criminal activities, which suggests that this has been a genuine regulation of Bitcoin. In addition, officials in the People's Bank of China have noted that Bitcoin exchanges operating in China needed strict administration and a form of licensing.

Tax

The other area in which establishments are progressively looking at how regulation will be implemented in respect of Bitcoin is in the area of tax. Due to the semi-concealment of Bitcoin, it can potentially be used to hide assets and assist in decreasing taxation. There is no uniform international approach on how profits made from trading in Bitcoin or other cryptocurrencies should be taxed. For example, the EU has declared that the trading of cryptocurrencies should not be subject to VAT on the basis that the exchange transactions were a supply of services rather than a supply of goods, which is an approach that was also taken by the UK prior to the EU ruling. In the US, the IRS confirmed in 2014 that it would treat cryptocurrencies such as Bitcoin as property instead of a currency. This means that any profits made from Bitcoin investment are charged at each investor's capital gains rate as opposed to their ordinary income rate.

Forthcoming Tactic

There are a number of potential tactics that specialists could take when it comes to the regulation of Bitcoin.

1. Cryptocurrency providers and exchanges will act as regulators of the currency by ensuring that AML and KYC regulations are complied with. Some of the standing exchanges, such as Coinbase, already enforce these regulations.
2. Governments could take the nuclear option and completely block Bitcoin, or other cryptocurrencies that don't abide by government regulation. As noted above, this would be difficult to enforce as governments have thus far found it difficult to completely block access to websites.
3. Governments could alternatively impose limited injunctions, such as forbidding the sale of real-life goods in exchange for cryptocurrency in order to avoid Bitcoin being used as imbursement for illicit goods.
4. Governments could also selectively standardize the industry, particularly in regards to taxation. This is similar to the current UK and EU approach. This would result in some of the important areas of the industry being synchronized, such as tax and AML, without widespread regulations being put in place.
5. Governments could deliver supporting mechanisms whereby the consent of users would implement their own 'community standards'. The problem associated with this approach

is that it may result in regulators allowing the illegal or fraudulent activity to go unchecked.

7.4 Possible future of cryptocurrencies

People seem to believe that cryptocurrency is on the verge of going mainstream because of this, expect to see the governments around the world establish new regulations that could lead to the centralization of coins like the Bitcoin which could stabilize and determine its value.

Others predict that all cryptocurrency transactions will are expected to be significantly reduced due to regulatory and security issues. That, however, does not mean that it is at its end. While not all cryptocurrency platforms will last, as long as they continue to solve problems and adapt, there will always be value in cryptocurrencies in the foreseeable future.

It is predicted that as more businesses decide that there is an opportunity in digital currency, the value will naturally rise with the demand. Current innovations such as bitcoin, Ethereum, and others that are just beginning for this technology that can help revamp many industries. There is plenty of opportunity in this space, will you be a part of it?

www.ingramcontent.com/pod-product-compliance
Lightning Source LLC
Chambersburg PA
CBHW021508210526
45463CB00002B/946